Poetry
Adventures

Poetry compilation by KS1 pupils

London

Edited by Lisa Adlam

This book was first published in Great Britain in 2014 by:

 Young**Writers**

Remus House
Coltsfoot Drive
Peterborough
PE2 9BF
Telephone: 01733 890066

Visit our website ...
www.youngwriters.co.uk

Printed and bound in the UK by BookPrintingUK
www.bookprintinguk.com

Foreword

Poetry Adventures is a competition specifically designed for Key Stage 1 children. The simple, fun introduction to narrative poetry gives even the youngest and least confident writers the chance to become interested in poetry by giving them a framework within which to shape their ideas. As well as this, it also allows older children to let their creativity flow as much as possible, encouraging the use of simile and descriptive language.

Given the young age of the entrants, we have endeavoured to include as many poems as possible. We believe that seeing their work in print will inspire a love of reading and writing and give these young poets the confidence to develop their literacy skills in the future.

Our defining aim at Young Writers is to nurture and encourage the talent of the next generation of authors. We are proud to present this latest collection of anthologies and hope you agree that they are an excellent showcase of young writing talent.

Contents

Let's go on the

Poetry
Adventures

Valentina And The Chocolate Factory

I took a bite of my chocolate bunny,
All of a sudden it spoke:
'Come in, don't be afraid,
Close the door and I'll take you on an adventure.'
So I crept inside and in a swirl and a twirl, I was off.
Then I landed in a tall man's arms.
'Oh my goodness, it's Willy Wonka!
I'm your number one fan!' I said excitedly.
Then he opened a door to a chocolate room.
'Taste a little of everything,' he said.
Then it got very late. There was no time to lose,
So we jumped in a car and all of a sudden,
I was back with my family.

Valentina Levi (6)

Annemount School, London

Safari Adventure

I was going on safari to see poisonous creatures
Because I love animals and all their features.
Then I saw a creature that was so big,
So I took a multicoloured photo of it.
Suddenly, a monster appeared
That had sharp teeth and a black beard.
He hunted the animals he wanted to eat.
He thought they were healthy and sweet.
So I took a pointy stick and threw it at the monster,
I saved the world and lived happily ever after.

Jahan Rostamyazdi (6)

Annemount School, London

1

Sea Adventure

I put on my swimsuit and dived into the sea.
I saw amazing creatures just like me.
I saw a shark covered in feathers,
I saw a clam with a gleaming pearl at the end of its tether.
In the sea I saw strange creatures with spikes on their backs,
I swam away before they attack.
I found beautiful coral that gleamed in the dark,
With only one shimmering, glimmering spark.
I saw rainbow jellyfish,
I saw starfish covered in red hearts.

Minnie Peters (6)

Annemount School, London

The Trash

T his morning I made a new friend,
H e lived in the trash
E ating the junk

T rash is as bad as me
R umble goes the monster's tummy
A ngry the monster is
S limy he is
H e is as bad as he lives.

Edward Dean (6)

Annemount School, London

Marshmallow World

In a magical place that no one knows,
There is a marshmallow world where marshmallows grow,
When I go there I see marshmallow lakes,
All of the bakers make marshmallow cakes.
Then I jump on a humongous bed,
Which turns into a marshmallow instead.
It's my favourite sweet, it's a soft and fluffy treat.
All of a sudden I see a marshmallow fairy,
She is kind and caring and not at all scary.
Then I fall down a marshmallow hole, but she gets me out. How?
With a magical marshmallow pole.
Then we discover the marshmallow world together,
I think she will be my best friend forever.

Maya Shergill (6)

Annemount School, London

The Beach

I went to a beach and got everything set up
I saw pinching crabs
I heard squawking seagulls
I smelled golden treasure
I ate delicious fish
I dug a hole in the sand
I ran, I ran, I jumped, I jumped
And a shark popped out,
Till I was home.

Max Tan (6)

Annemount School, London

3

On Safari

One day I went on holiday to a place I'd never been to,
I was excited because we were going to explore,
The whole land of Africa.
We had to take a big plane and drove down a lane.
We met some nice explorers who took us to the jungle.
I saw a tiger, a parrot and a rhino,
On safari.

Matthew Janowski (6)
Annemount School, London

The Gingerbread House

One day I drove in my blue car
To the forest and very far.
I saw a gingerbread house
My tummy said yum, yum, yummy.
There was even enough for my mummy.
I loved the soft chocolate chimney,
It was delicious in my tummy.
Then I ate lots of sweets,
They were my favourite treats.
I had a lovely time at the gingerbread house,
I would love to go back.

Kian Parvizi (6)
Annemount School, London

Crazy Land

I was walking down the road
When I fell down the throat of a toad.
It was Crazy Land because I saw Granny Ford.
Then I tamed an Enderman and I called it Fenton,
I climbed the colourful tree and saw my reflection in the sea.
I saw lots of baskets being lowered to the ground,
But down below they were nowhere to be found.
I saw LooLoo the snoo and he said, 'How do you do?'
Then I heard Mum shout it was time to go home,
I didn't mind because I was sick of playing alone.

Thomas James (7)

Annemount School, London

A Land That's New

Once I had a play date with my friend
I never wanted it to end
That day Benjamin led me to a trap door
We had never been there before
It led to a magical world
There were thousands of lollipop swirls
We met a dragon that breathed chocolate
And sat on a candy seat
We found a place filled with amazing sweets
We met the queen who was not a bit mean
She told us to plant some more sweet trees and gave us the seeds
We planted them all and sweets started to fall
All before it was time to go home.

Maya Cragg Hine (6)

Annemount School, London

5

The Castle

I went in my adventure cupboard one day
I saw a parcel right next to a castle
It said the castle needed one more soldier
But first I had to dodge a big boulder
It said the code was 1333, so I went through the door
There were angry guards
A hard brick floor
I dressed in armour
We put the boulder against the door
I ran upstairs and poured boiling hot goo on the bad soldiers
We saved the day.

Gleb Chalov (6)

Annemount School, London

The Land Of Wishing

This morning I chased Mr Rabbit down a hole
I arrived in Magical Land where no one knows
It's the land of wishing
I once wished for a rose
I wished for a monster called Who
I wished for a bing, bang, bong
I wondered why it was so long
I wished for a new friend called Mary
But she turned out to be quite scary
I wished for a blue dolphin
I wished for a piece of The Gingerbread Man
All because I was his biggest fan.

Roxie Peters (6)

Annemount School, London

6

The Blue Cloud Adventure

If you go to the sky, you will wonder why
Everything is blue and the queen is called Sue.
I once went there to see a blue baby bear
But I shrunk and became tiny,
There where the houses are blue and shiny.
I met a girl who wanted to go to the castle
But we had to take a present or a parcel.
We grabbed a blue mouse that was a present for Sue,
The rainbow we walked over
And the green was as bright as a clover.
We got to the castle and gave Sue her parcel
I said to the girl and Sue, 'This is a lovely land of blue.'
But in a swirl and a twirl I was at home and sadly alone.

Madeleine Curry (6)

Annemount School, London

Untitled

In a land that no one knows
Is where sweeties grow
I smell sweet, colourful flowers
I see a gang of dancing bees
Pink marshmallows
A dog made of chocolate and sugar
As brown as a log
And a tasty sweetie house.

Chiara Palazzesi (6)

Annemount School, London

Untitled

I went under my bed to find my toys
Instead I saw a magical forest full of joy
I quickly went to call my sister and brother
They came and followed me into the wood
We saw multicoloured birds
We saw a blue fox and squirrels that lived in a tree
I could hear birds singing away
It ended up being my favourite place to play
We swung on trees from one branch to another
And then I heard my older brother
'Let's stay, let's stay,' he said
So we made an enormous tent
By the end of the day we were completely spent!

Aarthi Raja (6)
Annemount School, London

Space

Space, space alien with me
I can see rocks, I can hear blocks,
I can smell rubbish cans,
I can feel a star.
Bumpty crash, bumpty crash,
A star bumped into space,
Bumpty crash, bumpty crash,
One of my bones broke.

Benny Berman (5)
Annemount School, London

Mermaid

Under the sea, under the sea,
Daddy comes with me.
I can see a mermaid,
I can hear bubbles popping.
I can swim in the sea
And suddenly I see a shark,
It comes close to me. *Argh!*

Amelie Rosen (6)
Annemount School, London

Under The Sea

Under the sea, under the sea,
I am a mermaid, that's me.
I have a friend as long as a pea,
She's a mermaid just like me.
Her name is Laylee.
She took me to a parade
And I saw her wonderful queen.

Jessica Townley (5)
Annemount School, London

Mermaid And Me

I had a sister and she had me.
She is a mermaid and we love having tea
Under the sea.
I met a mermaid, a mermaid under the sea.
She was as nice as me.
We went on a shark hunt,
I was scared but I will never forget that day!

Elen Johnson (6)
Annemount School, London

9

In The Forest

Chopping trees, me and my monkey
In the night I see a tree
And I hear the engine
And I feel the shaking.
I smell smoke and I taste animals.
I get to a tree and go to sleep.
When I wake up, I go hunting.

Elliot Curry (5)

Annemount School, London

Me And Tiger

Shh, shh, the jungle trees,
Halfway through there's a tiger.
He jumps and leaves come off the trees.
I jump backwards because I am scared.
But the tiger just wanted to be friends
And after a while we became like brothers in the jungle.
I rode on his back and we went hunting every day.

Elliot Wood (5)

Annemount School, London

Me And My Monkey

In the jungle I can see a monkey.
She thought that I was a mother monkey.
We went into the trees swinging from the vines
Shouting out funny rhymes.
Monkey and me
Monkey and me
In the jungle.

Baanoo Negahban (5)

Annemount School, London

Me And My Dog

I see lots and lots of trees
In the rainforest.
The dog and me swinging on vines
Smiling all the way.
I smell flowers and see tigers
Through the tree towers.

Edgar Tyne (5)
Annemount School, London

School Lunch

In the sea I see a shark eating a school of fish.
I am going to kill it because I am hungry.
I am going to eat it as school lunch.
I hear bubble bubble,
I am going to eat the shark because I am back at school.

Aki Blendis (6)
Annemount School, London

Under The Sea

Splash, splash, splash, under the sea,
Mermaid and me.
I can hear fish and sharks following me.
I can see sharks.
With the mermaid I swam through the sea.
I met a shark who wanted to eat me.
'Argh!' I said. 'No!'
He swam away and said, 'Sorry.'
I'll never forget the shark and me.

Lila O'Connor (5)
Annemount School, London

Space

I am going to space.
I am going with my snake.
I met an alien.
I had tea with him
And when I went home
I saw a bee.

Ayaan Hussain (6)
Annemount School, London

Rainforest

I am going with a tiger,
I can see a tree.
I can hear a tiger,
I can feel fur,
I can smell grass,
I can taste rain.
Sleepy, sleepy, the tiger,
Off I get.
Jump up!
I get ready for the adventure to start . . .

Gabriel Pereira-Mendoza (5)
Annemount School, London

The Two Mermaids' Adventure

Under the sea I saw a mermaid with me.
We became sisters of the sea.
If I swim away, so will my sister.
If there's a typhoon, my sister
Will get away under the sea.
It is fun.

Jasmine Wariebi (5)
Annemount School, London

The Snake And Me

Run through the jungle, snake and me,
I have the snake and he has me.
I go on him and then I hear a *pop,*
A cherry drop, yum yum in our tums!
We both went to find some plums.
Interesting, fascinating jungle I see,
The snake and me.

Freya Matthews (6)
Annemount School, London

Under The Sea

Under the sea, under the sea,
Sharks, whales, clownfish and me.
I can see the coral reef,
Seaweed, starfish, clams and more.
The great big sea, there is so much to see.

Sam James (6)
Annemount School, London

Under The Sea

Under the sea, under the sea
Ariel went with me.
I can see a clam shell.
I can hear bubbles.
I can feel water animals.
I can smell liquid.
I can taste salt.
Me and Ariel had a tea party with fish.
I will never forget this day.

Ruby-Rae Kemp (5)
Annemount School, London

Under The Sea

Under the sea, under the sea,
A scuba diver alien I can see.
He comes with me to see a tree,
I don't know why he came with me.
Well, he looked at the tree
And dived in the sea,
I dived too – *splash!*
We're in big, wavy water.
Argh! A shark!
I scream with horror,
The creatures will help,
But the creatures did help,
Honest they did.
Then I saw an octopus
And two colourful fish.
Let the adventures begin . . .

Toby Buchler (6)
Annemount School, London

Under The Sea

Bubble, pop, pop, a mermaid swims with me.
We had a party and then we went for tea
And then we watched TV.

Chloe Black (6)
Annemount School, London

15

Funfair

I put on my sparkling Sleeping Beauty dress,
I opened the magic door,
A friend came with me,
We saw a funny clown on a unicycle,
I heard birds singing,
I won a prize at the fair,
My friend was trying to win a prize.
We had dinner and lunch, it was delicious.
Then suddenly I saw a horse.
I was riding it while my friend finished her dinner.
We played on the swings.
We stroked a fluffy dog, it was nice.

Lola Christou (6)

Chingford CE Voluntary Controlled Infants' School, London

Going To The Moon

I went to the moon,
I went with SpongeBob.
I went in a rocket,
I smelled lovely, beautiful roses.
I heard people talking,
I explored the moon.
I had a picnic.
I helped a person,
I got home in a rocket.

Joe Hamandishe (6)

Chingford CE Voluntary Controlled Infants' School, London

Desert

I grabbed my magic carpet
And I went to the desert.
I went with my mum and dad and my sister.
I saw a brown camel and I played in the sand.
The ground shook. I looked up and saw a giant.
He was cooking a sheep on a campfire.
Then I made a sandcastle.
Suddenly, the door appeared.

Alex Carrannante (7)
Chingford CE Voluntary Controlled Infants' School, London

At School

I went to school and there was a secret door.
I went with Jess, Justin, a mermaid and a dog.
We went through a door.
Suddenly, we were in the sea.
We met an alien in the sea.
We felt safe and we saw baby whales.
We flew back home.

Priya Banerjee (7)
Chingford CE Voluntary Controlled Infants' School, London

The Best Adventure Yet

I went to the dark, gloomy forest,
I went with everyone from the Mickey Mouse Clubhouse,
A tiger was chasing us, he just wanted to say hello,
His name was Loopy Loo,
He joined us on the rest of our adventure,
We saw green nature,
Felt smooth plants in the green grass,
We got a colourful double-decker bus because it would take us home.

Grace Knott (7)

Chingford CE Voluntary Controlled Infants' School, London

Saudi Arabia

I went into a door in my house,
But when I opened it, a magic portal appeared,
So I went in then I was in Saudi Arabia.
I found my baby niece there.
When we went into a shop we saw a giant camel,
Then we ran out.

Sara Sharif (6)

Chingford CE Voluntary Controlled Infants' School, London

Going To The Moon

I went to the moon
And I wore my space helmet.
My mummy, daddy, brother and sister came too.
We met an alien who asked us
If we'd like to go to the park.
We said yes and had lots of fun.
Then we had to go home.
I said, 'Goodbye, I'll see you soon.'

Sophie Barry (7)
Chingford CE Voluntary Controlled Infants' School, London

Snowy Land

I put on my fluffy hat and a warm scarf
My mum and dad came with me
We went to a snowy land
We went by massive remote control plane
It was freezing
It was snowing
We made a snow dog
And put snow dust around his neck
He came alive
The magic dust was there
We got some out of his bag
And flew all the way home

Maisie Kneller (7)
Chingford CE Voluntary Controlled Infants' School, London

19

North Pole

I put my sparkly, long dress on.
I was walking and wasn't looking where I was going.
I fell down a hole.
It was dark and it took me to the North Pole.
I saw my mum and dad.
I didn't know they worked there.

Keira Martin (7)

Chingford CE Voluntary Controlled Infants' School, London

Rainforest

I put my blue, sparkly dress on,
I flew over Sweden to the rainforest.
I went with my brother.
I swung from tree to tree
And saw a massive kangaroo.
I heard a lion roaring.
Then suddenly we were in danger.
Every animal except monkeys and kangaroos chased us.
I just remembered my sparkly, blue dress.
I was glad that we escaped, thanks to the dress.

Amelie See (7)

Chingford CE Voluntary Controlled Infants' School, London

Crazy Land

I put my cape on and opened my magic door.
I saw a ship, they saw me and they got me on.
Then we sailed to Spain.
I got off and walked, then I saw a big dinosaur!
He was chasing me and was going very fast.
I tripped over a rock.
He picked me up and threw me into a pond!
It was not very nice at all.
I got out and dried myself, then I carried on.

Massimo Angeletos (7)

Chingford CE Voluntary Controlled Infants' School, London

The Island Trip

I went to a big island,
When I got there I had a tropical drink.
I got in a deep blue swimming pool.
I went to a big, colourful drinking bar
Where you could watch talent shows.
I went with my dog, Rex.

Emily Millward (7)

Chingford CE Voluntary Controlled Infants' School, London

Desert

I grabbed my magic carpet
And went to the desert.
On the way to the desert
I saw some animals;
A cheeky monkey swinging by,
A vicious tiger eating meat
And a singing bird.
Finally, I reached the desert.
It was very hot there.
I heard people building stuff.
I smelled camels.
I felt the yellow sand.

Oliver Green (6)

Chingford CE Voluntary Controlled Infants' School, London

The Rainforest

Before I went to the rainforest,
I put my blue coat on.
I was going to the rainforest.
I was going with Mum and Dad.
I saw a strong gorilla.
I heard a tweeting owl.
I climbed up a tree.
I made a coconut drink.
I slept with the monkeys.
Then I flew home.

Stella Hawkins (6)

Chingford CE Voluntary Controlled Infants' School, London

Sweety Land

I am going to sweety land
With a colourful, kind, gingerbread man
And his dog, Ginger.

We are really excited
Because we wanted to get our friend
Gingerbread man, new buttons.

We can hear sweety air falling like rain.
We can smell strawberry and chocolate flowers.
We got him some new jelly bean buttons.

Poppy Ryan-Law (6)
Chingford CE Voluntary Controlled Infants' School, London

My Magical Forest

Today I went to the forest
I took my dog, Lizzy.
When I got there
There was slushy mud.
There were flowers in the mud.
I let my dog off the lead.
She ran off into the slushy mud
She dug up the mud
And found a dinosaur bone.
She ate the dinosaur bone.
'Yum!' said the dog.

Ellie Smith (6)
Chingford CE Voluntary Controlled Infants' School, London

Jess Rose Travels To The Moon

There once lived a little girl called Jess Rose.
She wanted to zoom to the moon in her huge rocket.
So she went to the moon, eating a biscuit.
When she landed on the moon she met an alien.
The alien said hello to Jess Rose like this,
'Blob blob blob.'
The alien was very slimy and gooey.
The animals were scared of the alien
And hid safely behind Jess Rose.

Olivia Smith-Ekwegh (7)
Chingford CE Voluntary Controlled Infants' School, London

My Time At Beauty School For Now

One sunny day it was very funny
Because I went to beauty school . . .
I put lots of blusher on
I went with my friends Kiren and Arora
I smelt mushroom pizza
We also tasted sliced cake
Arora got to see a very special person
Who was a princess of happiness
And all of us heard her kitten Kit.

Isabella Pullum (6)
Chingford CE Voluntary Controlled Infants' School, London

The Adventure To Moshi Monster Land

The other day I chose to go to
Moshi Monster Fun Park.
I went with Moshi Deablear.
We went and we saw moshlings.
I heard people laughing, ha, ha, ha.
I felt the hot summer sun falling onto me.
I smelled the lovely flowers.
They smelled beautiful.

Jaime Spencer (6)
Chingford CE Voluntary Controlled Infants' School, London

My Dreams

Today I was a mermaid in the Portugal sea.
I travelled with Isabel, a dog called Anna,
Harry Styles and a dog called Elsa.
With my friends I went to the sea kingdom.
At the sea kingdom we met the sea king and queen.
For dinner I had chocolate cake.
The next day I got ready for the surfing competition.
We both dressed differently.

Matilda Roney (6)
Chingford CE Voluntary Controlled Infants' School, London

Beauty School

I went to beauty school
And put on blusher
And so did Lili and King Krin.
We smelled cheese pizza.
I had a rainbow.
We saw books.
We heard a kitten,
It was barking like a dog.
I now have rainbow hair.

Eleanor Taylor (6)
Chingford CE Voluntary Controlled Infants' School, London

Fun

I went to a Moshi Monsters Fun Park
With Em and Chloe.
I smelled flowers.
I felt very hot and it was fun
Because you could hear people laughing.
I ate juicy red berries.
There were fun and crazy places to go.
I saw beautiful flowers,
I went on a roller coaster.

Ella James (7)
Chingford CE Voluntary Controlled Infants' School, London

Rumbly Crazyland

Today I woke up and bumped into a tree.
I didn't remember my owner.
We had a big fight.
There were zombies chasing us.
We drove a car to Crazyland
And we were upside down.
We fell from the ceiling and we cried.

Luke Howlett (6)

Chingford CE Voluntary Controlled Infants' School, London

My Adventure To Beautiful School

At beautiful school there is a pool
I went with Chloe, 1D, Jessie J
And a cute husky dog.
I saw flowers and smelled daffodils.
Jessie saw a slippy flower slide.
All of us had super soup.
1D heard flowers swaying softly.
The flowers were sweeping.
All the teachers were teaching.
The grass was fresh,
Everyone wore a dress.
The butterflies were fluttering.

Libby Rogers (6)

Chingford CE Voluntary Controlled Infants' School, London

Magical Forest

I decided to take my crazy dog
To the foggy forest
And she smelled a tasty bone.
She saw a bright sun.
In the forest I felt pretty flowers
And I heard wavy waterfalls.
My dog and I had spicy sweets.
My dog is called Lizzy
And she has got fleas.
She is brown.

Jessica Bainborough (7)
Chingford CE Voluntary Controlled Infants' School, London

Adventure To Warm Spanish Sea

Last night I decided to go
With my pet Daydreaming Dolphin and Jessie J.
I tasted perfect pumpkin pie.
I felt the warm, calm sea on my toes.
Suddenly, I turned into a mermaid.
I found a lost, dizzy dog in the sea
And then I took him to my rock
To have a bone.

Isabel Wright (6)
Chingford CE Voluntary Controlled Infants' School, London

My Crazy Adventure

Today me and my dog, Fire,
Bumped into a tall tree.
Then Fire woofed at me
And we were in Crazy Wazy Land.
The sparkly lights shone on me.
We were upside down.
There were mouldy zombies
And smoky bottles of poison.
Cakes fell from the ceiling.
I caught a cake and it tasted yummy.
We fell and felt fluffy dogs.
I heard arrows getting fired.
Fire woofed and I gulped . . .

Louis Gillies (7)

Chingford CE Voluntary Controlled Infants' School, London

My Crazy Poem

One dark night I woke up
There was a time machine
We went to the dinosaurs
We could hear a waterfall
We tasted delicious doughnuts
We could feel baby Ipo's belly
We could eat popcorn
Fluffy candyfloss
And chocolate lollies
We could smell fish and chips
And coconut juice.

Carmen Kassai (7)

Chingford CE Voluntary Controlled Infants' School, London

Going To The Moon

Today I went to the silvery moon
I took my spotty bag
Izzy Wizzy, the cat, came too
Spotty dog chased the one-eyed alien
The cow jumped over the moon
I tasted an alien cake
I heard an alien talk
'Blob, blob, blob.'

Ruby Crook (6)
Chingford CE Voluntary Controlled Infants' School, London

A Day Out With David Tennant

On a rainy day
I went with David Tennant
To the jungle
To see how good he was at fighting
Then I saw K9
Who said hi
I was shocked
Then I saw a lot of smoke
I was scared
I ran away.

Reece Wilson (7)
Chingford CE Voluntary Controlled Infants' School, London

The Ninja Poem

Today I did decide
To go to Ninja Land
I went there with my dad and George
Crash! Bang! Boom!
We lived in the Ninja house
His werewolf guards attacked us
We were the good kings of the city
Then we saw millions of baddies.

Thomas Kennett (6)

Chingford CE Voluntary Controlled Infants' School, London

Going To The Moon

I zoomed to the moon
In a very fast rocket
And we landed with a bump
We had moon cake for tea
And we had fun.

Ashton Sharpe (6)

Chingford CE Voluntary Controlled Infants' School, London

My Magical Adventure

One bright sunny day
My sensible sister, cute dog, loving brother, Mum and Dad
We all slid down a rainbow
Suddenly, we all landed in a funky forest
It was a magical rainforest
I smelled summer flowers
Heard singing birds
Tasted chocolate cake
Felt excited
We explored for a bit
And we saw a wishing pond
We saw lots of things.

Summer Bruce (6)
Chingford CE Voluntary Controlled Infants' School, London

My Amazing Adventure

In the summer
I went to the deep, swaying sea
I went with Josie, Poppy and a mermaid
I went for a paddle in the sea
I met a koala bear and a panda
After a while, I saw a bit of coloured coral
I heard a very scary vampire with a pet lion
On a blistering hot summer's day I smelled a dying daisy
In the sea I felt rocky rock
I tasted a chocolate lollipop.

Lola Metcalfe (6)
Chingford CE Voluntary Controlled Infants' School, London

32

My Magical Adventure

On a hot summer's day
I decided to go out with Charlotte and Rose
We went to the seaside
I went in the wavy sea
When I put my head underwater
I could breathe underwater
I quickly told Rose and Charlotte
I told them the good news
I tasted lovely lollipops
I felt colourful coral
I saw a magical mermaid
I turned into a mermaid and I was excited.

Poppy Revoir (6)
Chingford CE Voluntary Controlled Infants' School, London

Spy

In a spooky forest
A dog with a wizzy owner
Said, 'Let's eat cockroach sandwich for lunch.'
Next he said, 'Let's go to Spy Land.'
They went with Michael Jackson
They danced and sang
They spied on the bad king.

Billy Ayto (6)
Chingford CE Voluntary Controlled Infants' School, London

Pirates

I put on my black jacket
On the ship is the Jolly Roger
We saw a skull
We took the treasure
So we found the gold.

Jack Smith (5)
Chingford CE Voluntary Controlled Infants' School, London

Pirate Adventure

I put on my pirate outfit
On the ship are a parrot and a monkey
We found an island with palm trees
We took the pirate ship
And we looked for the treasure
We found gold and rings.

Michael Woolf (6)
Chingford CE Voluntary Controlled Infants' School, London

Pirates

I put on my pirate outfit
On the ship are the pirates
We saw an island
There were skeletons with parrots
We took the map and we took the compass
And we walked through the weather
The treasure was gold with some diamonds
Hooray, we found the treasure.

Caitlin Roberts (6)
Chingford CE Voluntary Controlled Infants' School, London

Pirate Adventure

I put on my pirate hat
On the ship are pirates
We saw an X which marks the spot
We took the treasure map and a compass
And we looked for some treasure
The treasure was hidden on the island
So we found gold.

Leah Crook (5)

Chingford CE Voluntary Controlled Infants' School, London

I Put On My Clothes

I put on my clothes
And my pirate hat.
We found a skeleton and some treasure;
We took the treasure!

Annabel Bailey

Chingford CE Voluntary Controlled Infants' School, London

Pirates

I put on my black coat
The ship has pirates and a parrot
We saw an island
We took the map and compass
And we found treasure.

Trinity Wing (5)

Chingford CE Voluntary Controlled Infants' School, London

Pirates

I put on my blue jacket
On the ship are pirates
We saw an X marks the spot
We took the treasure map
And we looked for the treasure
The treasure was hidden on an island
So we found the treasure with gold.

Joshua Beaton (6)
Chingford CE Voluntary Controlled Infants' School, London

Pirate Adventures

I put on my jacket
On the ship are pirates
We saw a coin
We saw a shark
We got the golden jewels.

Skye Williams (5)
Chingford CE Voluntary Controlled Infants' School, London

Pirate Adventure

I put on my black jacket
On the ship was Captain Hook
We saw a shark, we grabbed him
So we found and took the treasure.

Mia Baker-Edmonds (6)
Chingford CE Voluntary Controlled Infants' School, London

Poetry Adventures

I put on my pirate outfit
On the ship are the captain and crew
We saw an island
We took the treasure
And we looked for gold coins
The treasure was far, far away
So we found lots of gold and skeletons.

Kieran-Lei Tavares (6)
Chingford CE Voluntary Controlled Infants' School, London

Pirates

I put on my blue jacket
On the ship are pirates and a monkey
We saw palm trees
We took the compass and a treasure map
And we looked for gold treasure
The treasure was gold
So we found treasure.

Ellie Buck (6)
Chingford CE Voluntary Controlled Infants' School, London

Pirate Adventure

I put on my black jacket
On the ship was a skull and crossbones
We saw an island
We took the compass
So we found gold.

Thomas Cockerell (5)
Chingford CE Voluntary Controlled Infants' School, London

Pirate Adventure

I put on my suit jacket
On the ship are the captain and crew
We saw an island
We took the treasure to the ship
The treasure was gold and silver
And all different colours
And we saw gold gold dust and silver gold dust
And a red ruby necklace.

Darcey McGillicuddy (6)

Chingford CE Voluntary Controlled Infants' School, London

Pirate Adventure

I put on my hat
On the ship are my gang
We saw a shark
We took the treasure
So we found a pirate to walk the plank.

Reef Stacey (5)

Chingford CE Voluntary Controlled Infants' School, London

Pirate Adventure

I put on my pirate outfit
On the ship are the captain and my crew
We saw an island for treasure
We took the treasure map
And we looked for treasure
The treasure was on an island
So we found gold.

Ben Harris (5)
Chingford CE Voluntary Controlled Infants' School, London

My Adventure Poem

I am a party girl.
I put my costume on.
I went to the ball.
I danced with the prince.
I made an accident by standing on his toe.
'I am a genius,' said the prince.
I had fun with the prince.
I had a drink with the prince.
Finally I got home.
I am a party girl.
PS I lost my shoe!

Lily-Mae Thorpe (6)
Chingford CE Voluntary Controlled Infants' School, London

My Adventure Poem

I am a little pig.
I put on my costume.
I built my house of bricks.
I went to visit my friend's house next door and I had fun.
Then we went into the garden and we picked some flowers.
I am a little pig!

Kayla Brennan (5)
Chingford CE Voluntary Controlled Infants' School, London

My Adventure Poem

I am a little pig.
I put my costume on.
I built my house of sticks.
I played in my house.
I go to my brother's house.
I play piggy in the middle.
I have fun.
I have a drink.
I am a little pig!

Isabella Cox (6)
Chingford CE Voluntary Controlled Infants' School, London

My Adventure Poem

I am the birthday boy!
I put my pyjamas on.
I sleep in my bed.
I have a badge.
I saw the three bears with Goldilocks.
I have a birthday cake.
I hope that my wishes come true.

Leo Van Woerkom (6)

Chingford CE Voluntary Controlled Infants' School, London

My Adventure Poem

I am a spider.
I put on my costume.
I was sitting on a web.
A lizard chased me.
Finally I got it.
I ate a fly.
Suddenly the whole place started to fall down.
I am a spider!

Jake Friend (6)

Chingford CE Voluntary Controlled Infants' School, London

My Adventure Poem

I am little Miss Muffet.
I put on my costume.
I went to a lovely field.
I am gone.

Greis Alia (5)
Chingford CE Voluntary Controlled Infants' School, London

My Adventure Poem

I am a mouse.
I put on my costume.
I went under the ground.
My friend is a dolphin.
We played football.
We followed a star.
I am a mouse.

Alfie Edmans (5)
Chingford CE Voluntary Controlled Infants' School, London

My Adventure Poem

I am a bear.
I put on my costume.
I went to the dark forest.
I found goldfish.
I ate the fish.
I am a bear.

Flynn Tierney (6)
Chingford CE Voluntary Controlled Infants' School, London

My Adventure Poem

I am Jill.
I put on my costume.
I went up the big hill with Jack.
I fell down the big hill and sat on a box of treasure.
I am Jill.

Ella Taylor (6)
Chingford CE Voluntary Controlled Infants' School, London

My Adventure Poem

I am Mr Punch.
I put on my costume.
I went to play.
My mum found out.

Benjamin Randolph Isaiah Clark (5)
Chingford CE Voluntary Controlled Infants' School, London

My Adventure Poem

I am Little Bo Peep.
I put on my costume.
I look for my sheep.
'Where have you been?' said Little Bo Peep.
I am Little Bo Peep.

Lucie Rodrigues (6)
Chingford CE Voluntary Controlled Infants' School, London

My Adventure Poem

I am a sheep.
I put on my costume.
My face is black.
I went to the house and I saw my brother and my sisters.
I am a sheep.

Martha Lumsden (5)
Chingford CE Voluntary Controlled Infants' School, London

My Adventure Poem

I put my costume on.
I go to the big forest.
I find a wood pet.
I am a bear.

Jayden Rasit (5)
Chingford CE Voluntary Controlled Infants' School, London

My Adventure Poem

I am a black cat.
I put on my costume.
I ran in the creepy wood.
I found some food.
I found my brothers.
I am a black cat.

Sophie Clayton (5)
Chingford CE Voluntary Controlled Infants' School, London

My Adventure Poem

I am a bear and I am big.
I put my costume on.
I go into the forest.
I am a bear.

Frank Laslett (6)
Chingford CE Voluntary Controlled Infants' School, London

My Adventure Poem

I am a sheep.
I put on my costume.
In the morning I ran to the dark forest.
I found another sheep.
I am a sheep.

Darcie-Belle Luxford (6)
Chingford CE Voluntary Controlled Infants' School, London

My Adventure Poem

I am a mouse.
I put on my costume.
I found cheese.
I am a mouse.

Zachariah Somerville-Banfield (5)
Chingford CE Voluntary Controlled Infants' School, London

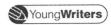

My Adventure Poem

I am a big, bad wolf.

I put on my costume.

I gobbled the pigs up

I feel sick.

I went to a party

I am a big, bad wolf.

Archie Block (6)
Chingford CE Voluntary Controlled Infants' School, London

My Adventure To Crazyland

I put on my funny Mr Bean costume.
I got there by digging underground.
I went to Crazyland.
I went with Michael Jackson.
I saw everything upside down.
I heard lovely birds chirping.
I felt smooth CDs.
I tasted scrummy chocolate.
I found a street.
I saw a grassy garden.
I had spaghetti bolognese.
I was full up.
So I roly polyed home on the stone path.

Alex Horder (6)
Chingford CE Voluntary Controlled Infants' School, London

Castle Poem

I went into the castle.
The walls felt cold.
I smelled chicken on the cooker.
When I went downstairs,
I saw a monster looking at me.
The monster was very scary,
So I got a big square
And it landed on the monster's head.
Then I cut the monster's head with my sword
Then the monster died
Then lunch was ready
So that was the end.

Kofi Gyem-Richards

High View Primary School, London

Castle

I can see water falling down,
I can smell yummy food,
I go to the spooky castle.
I can taste cake.
A bad skeleton will come
And I will fight it.
A zombie will come
And I will put it in the dungeon.
That's the end.

Nikita Kamble (5)

High View Primary School, London

A Castle Adventure

I go into a spooky castle with spider webs,
The walls feel smooth.
I taste chicken.
I can hear the wind blowing,
I see a zombie in the dungeon.
Then I shot him, then lived happily ever after.
I got married and became a king.

Shamar Grant (6)

High View Primary School, London

A Castle Adventrue

I go into the spooky castle.
The walls are like a rock.
I look at the skeletons.
I can eat the pizza.
The skeletons walk.
I get the spooky skeletons in my booby trap.
It was fire and is the end of the stalks.

Adnan Hazel (6)

High View Primary School, London

A Castle Adventure

I am going to the scary castle.
In the castle there is a skeleton.
I am going to throw a net on the ghost
Because he is spooky.
Now I am going home.

Batool Boakye (5)
High View Primary School, London

A Castle Adventure

I go into the castle
I can see a beautiful princess
I was so excited
I forgot what I was doing.
I don't know if someone
Is going to rescue me.
All of a sudden, someone came.

Cleo Cookson (6)
High View Primary School, London

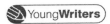

A Castle Adventure

I am going into the castle.
I can smell smelly socks.
I can see a skeleton.
I can hear creepy spiders.
It is cold like ice.
We can throw the net over.
I am going home for dinner.

Leland Pearson (6)

High View Primary School, London

A Castle Poem

I go into the spooky castle.
It smells like a scary skeleton.
I feel the walls,
They are as freezing as ice.
It is very dark.
Suddenly, a ghost appears.
I get on my horse and ride away
And never went there again.
That was the end of everything.

Elaina Holmes (6)

High View Primary School, London

A Castle

I go in a castle
I can see Rapunzel,
She is in a window.
The castle feels ice cold.

Sharika Bhuiyan (5)

High View Primary School, London

A Castle Adventure

Our castle is spooky.
I can smell smoke.
I can feel the cold stones.
I can hear a wolf.
I can taste chicken.
I can see vampires.

Jaydyn Smith (5)
High View Primary School, London

Castles

I go into my zombie castle
I see a vampire.
I am brave.
I see a vampire
And I shoot an arrow.
He is dead.
I run away.

Chester Hall (6)
High View Primary School, London

A Castle Adventure

I go into the castle
I hear a banging noise
It is a skeleton
And I attack it.
I see the king and queen
I see an ugly skeleton.
I throw a net over its head
And that is the end of him.

Rosemarie Navarro (6)
High View Primary School, London

A Castle Adventure

I go to the spooky castle.
The walls feel warm.
I can see a skeleton.
He is walking in the castle.
He hid but I found him
And killed him.

Kaluba Dyer (5)
High View Primary School, London

Castle Poem

The castle is old.
It smells like rotten fish.
The drawbridge was blown away
But we get back safe and sound.

Ronnie Pearce-Godfrey (6)
High View Primary School, London

The King's Stolen Treasure

In the dark castle
The knight stole the treasure
From the king.
The king got it back,
The queen had seen the gold.
The queen liked dancing.
The king got the queen's ring back
In a sack wearing a mac.

Nevaeh Wright (6)
High View Primary School, London

The Swimming Pool

I love the swimming pool
When it's hot it keeps me cool
Being underwater is where I love to be
Wearing swimming goggles so that I can see.
Indoor or outdoor in the sun
I love to go with my family and have lots of fun.
I love to do jumps and make a splash
Sink down to the bottom and then rise up in a flash.

Ryan Francis Barry (5)

Holy Family Catholic Primary School, London

Disneyland

I am planning to go to Disneyland
My friends Hiroto, Tate and Ryota all spoke of it.
I want to explore the land.
I want my dad to drive under the gate
With the words overhead 'Disneyland'.
I want to ride on a train
Have lunch in a diner.
I want to see all the characters
As I know them from television.
I want to spin around in teacups
And never feel like enough.
To me this is the happiest place on Earth
Where all the cash is worth.

Ali Assi (6)

Holy Family Catholic Primary School, London

53

Up In The Sky

A Lego man was found
His name was Jan.
He loved to run.
I took him in and gave him some drink.
He drank it all and let me build more.
His hands were red
And his face was wet.
We all shouted out then he fell apart.

Jan Rybarczyk (6)
Holy Family Catholic Primary School, London

Adventure Antarctica

Daniel and me had a swim in the sea
On the seabed we found a trapdoor
And when we opened the secret door
There was a whole new world to explore!
A beautiful blue sea with seaweed
And orange fish appeared in front of us.
Suddenly, a swordfish jumped out of the shoal
And chased us to the shore with mountains.
When we climbed to the top, we found a treasure chest full of gold.

Oscar Sherbrooke (6)
Holy Family Catholic Primary School, London

We Will Climb A Mountain

We will see lots of colourful birds singing.
Suddenly, we heard bells ringing.
We saw a magic castle on the top of the hill,
We opened a magic door and saw Rapunzel
Having a big meal.
We were dancing around the castle.
It was fun.
We were done.
We had to go home,
We had a very good time.

Natasha Zielak (6)
Holy Family Catholic Primary School, London

Me And Pokémon's Adventure

Me and Pokémon went to space
Then the moon was kind and sweet.
We could see lots of cheese,
We could hear the lovely wind.
We were very excited.
We could smell tasty burgers.
We had yummy hot chocolate.

Nisrine Cotter (5)
Holy Family Catholic Primary School, London

Five Little Senses In The Tank

Goldfish, goldfish, what can you see?
I can see a face in the shimmering water
Looking at me.
Loach fish, loach fish, what can you hear?
I can hear running filter bubbling in my ear.
Rainbow fish, rainbow fish, what can you taste?
I can taste the fish food pellets sinking away.
Blue fish, blue fish, what can you smell?
I can smell a smelly fishy fish all around me.
Little girl, little girl, what can you feel?
I can feel a fish's scales rubbing my skin.
Fish tank, fish tank, what do you sense?
I sense everyone in here!

Myriam Grant (6)

Holy Family Catholic Primary School, London

Sweety Boy

There's a boy with his parents,
off to find some sweets.
There's a magic land with black lollipops,
candy canes and treats.
There's a sweety bird in magic land,
whistling away.
There's a river made of melted chocolate
to swim in every day!

Enzo Zeballos (5)

Holy Family Catholic Primary School, London

Dream

I went on the magic train to the magic playground.
My mummy and Miss Martin were with me.
I saw a witch and she turned the playground into a gooey house.
There were spider webs and a smelly tree.
I felt a rotten leaf, then I woke up!

Wojtek Kowalkiewicz (6)
Holy Family Catholic Primary School, London

Going To The Jungle

I am going to the jungle with my mummy.
I can hear a noisy tiger, my ears hurt.
I can smell a smelly hippopotamus.
I can feel a rough tree.
I can taste an apple, mm, yummy!
The cheetah started to be hungry,
He ate a zebra. It was scary!

Mar Perez Soler (6)
Holy Family Catholic Primary School, London

Magic Sweetshop Land

I took Dad and Mum and brothers to Magic Sweetshop Land,
Dad bought chocolate ice cream one hundred
And Mum bought chocolate necklaces.
Mum's necklaces have gone and Dad's chocolate ice cream has gone.

Ryota Nakamura (6)
Holy Family Catholic Primary School, London

Two Sweet Little Girls

Two little girls went on an adventure
Following the candyfloss cloud of pink.
Sofia cried, 'Ooh!' and Lilly pointed,
'That river is chocolate I think!'
The trees were made of strawberry gum.
'Please can we have some?'
Asked Sofia and Lilly with glee.
'I think that smells of liquorice,
Let's climb up and see.'
Two little girls with bellies full as can be.
'I feel ill, I think that grumbling sound is me.'
Let's go home, this sweet adventure has been fun.

Sofia Bhaloo (6)

Holy Family Catholic Primary School, London

Pirate Land

The pirate went into the sea
His big ship is called Julie.
He sailed on a hot day
It was the end of May.
Three friends joined him
Their names were Ben, Liz and Kim.
The naughty pirate says a lot
'I'm the best and you are not.'
The ship sailed to Pirate Land
Looking for gold hidden in the sand.
They ate pizza on their way
And when they arrived they said hooray!

Jovan Michail (5)

Holy Family Catholic Primary School, London

Magic Chocolate Cake Land

I went to the magic chocolate cake land,
With Adonay, Leon, baby Yafet and my dad,
In the magic chocolate cake land,
We saw a sweetie sweet,
And a chocolate fountain,
We heard a windy wind,
We tasted chocolate cake,
We felt a chocolate fountain,
We smelt a baked cake,
Finally, all the chocolate cake was going to be finished,
And it was going to be closed.

Jonathan Mulugeta (5)
Holy Family Catholic Primary School, London

Fat Cat

There's a fat cat
Sitting on a mat and snoring.
Dreaming about a fly
Flying in the sky.
The cat wants the fly as a snack.
Then he woke up and screamed,
'That was only a dream!'

Alicia Nedza (6)
Holy Family Catholic Primary School, London

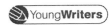
The Tooth Fairy Land

The tooth fairy couldn't find any baby teeth.
Then the pixie dust put ten baby teeth into her bag.
Then all the fairies gathered into a circle
And sang a beautiful song.

Molly Copelin (5)
Holy Family Catholic Primary School, London

Legoland

Santa will be the best in Legoland,
When I go there the reindeer stand,
All together.
In snowy weather,
Shiny and bright,
Twinkling light.
We throw snowballs at each other,
Paul, Shanice and me and my mother.
It was really lots of happy fun,
Going home I fell asleep,
My day was done.

Angel Laughton (5)
Holy Family Catholic Primary School, London

Me And The Animal

Me and the animal went to see,
The big bird in the huge tree.
I had seen everything from the top of the tree,
I looked everywhere to see the chocolate house,
The blue sky shining above the sun,
The animal was a purple lion.
He was nice to me,
I like to ride on the lion!

Lola White (6)
Holy Family Catholic Primary School, London

Swimming

Mummy, sister Ola and me went for a swim
And Daddy drove us in the car quick.
The water was cold, but we were brave
And we went in anyway.
We swam fast and had fun.
Mummy said we are going home,
But we said 'No, no, no!'
Daddy said 'Restaurant,'
And I said, 'Yum, yum, yum!'

Magda Banas (6)
Holy Family Catholic Primary School, London

Disney World

Walking through Disney World,
What can I see?
The shimmering and beautiful princess.
Walking through Disney World,
What can I hear?
The nice princess singing.
Walking through Disney World,
What can I feel?
The princess's hand.
Walking through Disney World,
What can I smell?
The delicious food.
Walking through Disney World,
What can I taste?
The scrumptious fish fingers.

Satoko Liddell (5)
Holy Family Catholic Primary School, London

First Me And My Family Went To Legoland

First me and my family went to Legoland.
Next my dad took me in a balloon.
After, we saw Mickey Mouse.
Then Mickey Mouse told me all about Legoland.
There are four Legoland parks around the world.
They are in Denmark, England, Germany and the USA.

Leon Dereje (5)
Holy Family Catholic Primary School, London

In Search Of The Golden Jewel

Our adventure started underwater.
We looked in caves,
We searched all around,
Even in the octopus ground.
We could not find the lovely jewel
Even after following the sunbeams.

The last place we looked
Was the sea palace and coral reef.
We found our golden jewel
Far below the light.

Tate Onraet (6)

Holy Family Catholic Primary School, London

Untitled

I see a castle with a big door,
Flags, windows, blocks.
What am I looking for?
I would like to go there with my friends,
To find Ben 10 who's got powerful watches.
I see Ben 10, a boy.
I hear the machine that makes his toy.
I feel a draught on my face.
I smell sweet chocolate in the air.
I see Ben 10 coming to me.
It is time for adventure and fun.
Me, my friends and number 10 boy.

Dawid Pielech (6)

Holy Family Catholic Primary School, London

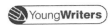
Magic Land

In the big castle in the magic land
Lives funny monster with his happy band.
A monster is happy when the wind is blowing
And making a chocolate cake when the sun is shining!
When I finished writing about the magic land
The castle turned into a big book full of sweets
Which I grab in my hand!

Karol Oyrzanowski (6)
Holy Family Catholic Primary School, London

The Colours

The apple is red and green
The sky is blue and white
The candle is red and orange
The leaf is green
The door is brown
The bird is white and black
The mud is brown
The cloud is blue
The wind is white
The rainbow is colourful
I like the rainbow.

Hiroto
Holy Family Catholic Primary School, London

Me And Ariel Wanted

Me and Ariel wanted to go on a hunt
To find the golden treasure chest.
The chest was glittering and sparkling
Full of gold and silver.
Ariel's fin was shiny.

Anastasia Panovic (6)
Holy Family Catholic Primary School, London

Angus, Grandpa And Me

Angus, Grandpa and me
Went for a walk by the deep blue sea.
The wind was freezing against my face
As me and Angus set off at a pace.
On the hard, wavy sand
We took some shells home,
My favourite looked like an eye.
I paddled in the sea with my toes squished in the sand,
I scooped up some water in the bottle in my hand.
'Shall I drink it?' I asked.
'No!' said Angus. 'No!' said Grandpa.
I thought I would give it a go. Yuck!
I won't do that again soon.
After a lovely day it was time to go home.
We walked back to the car smiling.

Daisy (5)
Holy Family Catholic Primary School, London

Sweety Palace

At the sweety palace
There lived a Princess called Alice.
She had a ginger kitten
She called it Paper Mitten.
They brought sparkly, sticky marshmallows
And gooey, mushy toffees.

Abigail (5)
Holy Family Catholic Primary School, London

Lego Adventure

I can feel water
I can touch water
I can taste chocolate
I can see Daddy
I am scared of the water.

Sam Gholamian (6)
Holy Family Catholic Primary School, London

The Canadian Princess

Me and Sophie went to save the Canadian princess
A wicked witch came and locked her in a cage
She cried and cried and cried.

Indie Schley-De Meur (6)
Holy Family Catholic Primary School, London

Winter In Poland

Two weeks ago I went to Poland with my family.
There was a lot of snow.
I saw snowy hills and blue sky.
We sat on the ice.
The ice was really cold and smooth.
We had a long walk and were hungry.
We had lunch on the top of the hill.
I ate sushi.
It was the best time ever.

Wiktor Kukla (5)

Holy Family Catholic Primary School, London

The Chocolate City

Once, there was a chocolate city with chocolate people.
The city had many chocolate faces and a chocolate eagle.
They had a chocolate river but one winter it disappeared,
Never to be seen . . . ever.

Callum Kusi-Appiah (5)

Holy Family Catholic Primary School, London

Untitled

Mum, Dad and I planned a summer trip to Disneyland.
We played with Mickey Mouse in the big Disney Clubhouse
And had fun.

Shauna (6)

Holy Family Catholic Primary School, London

Rainbows, Birds And Butterflies

Butterflies and birds happy as can be,
Flying happily and free in the morning breeze.
The rainbow is so colourful,
Red, pink and blue,
I would love to dance on the rainbow with you.
The rainbow is colourful as can be,
It makes my eyes shine and my face smiley.

Rachel Elroy (6)
Holy Family Catholic Primary School, London

Sea Lab

Underwater, deep down,
A lab is there.
Sea creatures are hearing *Boom! Pop! Bang!*
Where Oscar and Daniel are doing experiments,
And lots of stuff happens to Oscar,
Because Daniel is the experiments maker.
Oscar is the one that gets tested on.

Daniel Duczmal (6)
Holy Family Catholic Primary School, London

The Sailing Leaf Boat

Sailing along on a green leaf boat
Passing bouncing frogs
Gold, shiny fishes
Butterflies flying around
Dreaming of a faraway land.

Caity McDonald (6)
Horniman Primary School, London

The Toad's Adventure

They saw a fluffy cloud,
It went in the sky
And the toad and the lolly jumped
From candy to candy
Then saw a magical land.
Hop, hop, hop,
Up the rainbow we go.
Sliding down the rainbow,
At the bottom of the rainbow
The toad meets a lollipop.

Jacob Waters (7)
Horniman Primary School, London

The Short Adventure

I caught a ride with a huge song thrush,
We glided magically over the high waves in a rush.
We saw fairies on a rainbow and I realised
It was a roadshow.

Briony Buckney (7)
Horniman Primary School, London

Sweet Adventure

I slid down Candy Mountain,
Flew across a sugar desert.
I came across a lollipop
Which led me to candy crush.
I ran up to a candy cane
And fell asleep.

Olivia Mardling (6)
Horniman Primary School, London

Leap, Hop, Leap

Hop, hop, hop, leap, leap, leap,
I got a toy and hitched a ride.
I am nearly there,
I rolled down a hill,
Roll, roll, roll. I'm here!

Rebecca Finders (6) & Sam Stagg (7)
Horniman Primary School, London

The Frog Found A Stone

The frog found a stone
We flew over a mountain
And glided over a desert
And then we glided down
And saw a stone.
We picked it up
And it was cold and frosty.

Charlie Eyles (6)
Horniman Primary School, London

Sole Taker

There was a kid called Kid
He swooped off a roller coaster
Into a rainbow at top speed
Sliding down a rainbow
With a key in his hand
And a black crow glided down
And took the key.

Zachary Wright (7)
Horniman Primary School, London

The Man Went On The Bird!

We flew on a bird
We went past a pond
We went across a road past a cone
Until we got to the phone.

Finn Miller Robinson (6)
Horniman Primary School, London

The Sticky Candy Cane

We hopped on a cloud
To a faraway place
Where candy canes were
We ate every candy cane
They were sweet, sticky and delicious.

Maisie Eyles (6)
Horniman Primary School, London

Midget John

John made a DIY jet pack
Flying round and round
Up and down.
A snow leopard
Appears on the mountain
And jumps on!

Joseph Steer (7)
Horniman Primary School, London

A Peregrine Falcon's Life

The peregrine falcon it glided
And slid across a car
And bolted straight through
The barred gate of the park.
He got kicked by a football
And flew all the way to Mexico city.
A baby volcano was just beginning to grow.

Silvester Alexandru
Horniman Primary School, London

The Seed

We sailed on a fluffy cloud,
We are trying to get to a faraway land.
We found a seed on the ground,
It grew and grew.

Hanai Gordon (7)
Horniman Primary School, London

In Space

I went to a rocket station
Then I went in the rocket
Next the rocket lifted off
And landed on the moon
And I explored the moon.

Rafael Woodhead Tavio (5)
Little Ealing Primary School, London

Fairy Land

In fairy land it was wonderful,
It was so wonderful because
They took me to the queen
And the princess and the king.
The queen was ill but the princess said
'You can have some tea with me.'

Sophia Jain
Little Ealing Primary School, London

Fairy Land

I flew with the fairies
To a castle.
We met the king and queen.
Then we found a hole in the ground.

Charlotte Hobern (6)
Little Ealing Primary School, London

I Went To The Dino Land!

Once I really wanted a dinosaur
But my mum said no.
I went out at night.
When it was one o'clock
I went back home
But the dino was a T-rex
And it woke my mum and dad up.
Then I quickly chased it.

Aubrey Noguera (6)
Little Ealing Primary School, London

I Went To London

I went to London Zoo
And we went to the swimming pool.
It had waterfalls.
We splashed my dad in his eye.
We laughed and laughed till sunset.
We met Eva.
We went home.

Beatrice Tovey (5)
Little Ealing Primary School, London

I Went To School

I went to school.
The new teacher was a fire dinosaur!
It was supposed to be a human.
I'm very happy with this.
It was my dinosaur, he's very bad.
Our usual teacher said, 'What on earth is this?'
'It's our teacher,' said the children.
'But I'm your teacher! Get out of here right now!
I'm serious,' said the teacher. 'Or I'll call the police.'
She did . . . but the dinosaur slapped the policeman.

Amine Tagnit Hammou (6)
Little Ealing Primary School, London

Fairyland Adventure

I went to Fairyland and saw a castle.
It was sparkling so much.
The fairies made some cakes for me
And they were delicious.
All the things were sparkling.
And I saw some mushrooms
And they were poisonous,
but one of them you could eat.
Something happened.
It was like a bang but it was a pop.

Alice McConnell (5)
Little Ealing Primary School, London

The Adventure

I went to the zoo
I had fun
I went to a jungle
I went to the lake
I went to the beach
I went to the park
I went to the sea.

Mila Roberts
Little Ealing Primary School, London

The Police

I went to a police station
And I drove a police car
And shot out of the window.
Then I jumped out of the door
And ran home.
I was sitting with my mum and dad.

Jack Procter-O'Malley (6)
Little Ealing Primary School, London

Disappearing Moshis

One day I went to Moshi Land with my mummy.
I saw some cute moshlings shouting.
I smelt some fleas, then the moshlings disappeared!
I called my mum to come and help look for them.
Finally, I found them in a tree house!
Then we had a picnic with ice cream.

Harriet Earle (5)
Little Ealing Primary School, London

Untitled

The baddies chased me into the shopping centre
And then I slept with 'Wreck It Ralph'.
Then next day it was Fix It Felix 30th anniversary.

Buddy (6)
Little Ealing Primary School, London

Off To Zombie Land

Once upon a time
I was off to Zombie Land.
When I was in Zombie Land,
I wanted to eat.
But I didn't have any food.
But my friend Good Zombie had some.
When we had our lunch,
We saw a robot zombie.
When me and my friend were fighting,
We won then we went home.

Jakub Osuch (6)
Little Ealing Primary School, London

The Space Adventure

Lorcan and me went into space
We packed up a mat and a hat
We had a picnic.
I could taste food.
I could see planets.
I could hear aliens.
We were having so much fun.
Suddenly, a ginormous alien
grabbed Lorcan.
I fought and I fought,
I threw a yo-yo on the monsters.
Lorcan fell and I caught him.
We went back into the space rocket.

Kalina Blackwood (6)
Little Ealing Primary School, London

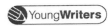
Magic Space

One day I was going out.
I got a sweet then I went to the park.
Then I went to space
And played with my family.
Then an alien took me and my family home.
We had tea.

Theo Wild (6)
Little Ealing Primary School, London

Sweety Adventure

I went to Sweety Land
It was quite a feety land
A sugar monster tried to eat me
But I fried his head off.
I ran away
The monster laid some hay
I jumped in the hay
It was prickly.
Ouch!
The monster put me in his pouch
I jumped out
The monster sent a scout
The scout told the monster.
I ran home
I saw a garden gnome.

Thomas Warren (5)
Little Ealing Primary School, London

An Adventure With Morris

Before I went on my amazing adventure,
I packed up my backpack
Because if I didn't, I wouldn't have any food.
When I was there I had my food,
Then I went in my car with Morris,
But the car went wrong.
Then we fixed it.

Cassius Khorsandi-Reilly (6)
Little Ealing Primary School, London

My Very Exciting Day

On Monday 18th February
I went to the colourful Sugar Rush.
My best friends came too.
I brought my cute pup too.
Some of my friends bought tasty cupcakes
For the journey.
We finally got in the big fast car,
Then we got there.
First me and my friends saw chocolate and sweets,
Then we heard people eating yummy sweets.
We felt melted chocolate,
We smelled tasty sweets and ate chocolate!
But then a big Sugar Monster quickly turned me into chocolate!

Iona Lewis Roythorne (6)
Little Ealing Primary School, London

My Journey

Once I climbed a high mountain
And I found some treasure.
It made me fly into the sky.
Suddenly, I landed on a small rock.
So I walked to a creepy forest,
Then a ghost popped out.

Next, we went to the park.

Sofia Roussel (6)
Little Ealing Primary School, London

The Water Slide

When I was going to school,
I saw a shiny key.
I touched the key,
Then me and Cameron vanished to Germany.
In the swimming pool,
Me and Cameron went down the big slide.
We bumped into somebody.

Samuel Hagger (5)
Little Ealing Primary School, London

Pyramid Adventure

I was on an adventure.
I saw a pyramid and I went in.
There was a mummy.
He started to chase me
And he wanted to eat me.
I climbed up the pyramid
And he didn't know where I was,
So I ran away.

Adam MAruf (6)

Little Ealing Primary School, London

The Jungle

One day me and my dad went into the jungle.
We saw a tiger and he started to chase us home,
But we shut the door.
We did not know he was good,
So we let him in and found out he was good,
So we kept him.

Uma James (6)

Little Ealing Primary School, London

81

Albania

One sunny day in Albania,
Cos it hardly ever rains,
I went to the seaside
And heard the waves splash.
I felt the fresh, blue sea
Coming closer and closer.
My two guinea pigs got splashed.
Holly and Imogen were laughing so much,
They needed to go to the toilet.

Marissa Merxhani (6)
Roehampton Church School, London

The Camping Trip

One sunny day we made some hot barbecue food.
I slept on a mattress.
In the afternoon we slept.
Dad was very mad at me for stealing some food.
Mum was done making the food,
My dad said, 'Let's have more!'
By the time we went I had eaten loads of ice cream.
I ate chicken, burgers and ice cream.

Ezaz Mahmood (7)
Roehampton Church School, London

Untitled

Today I am going to swim
With my mum and my brother.
My cousin got her swimming costume.
I had fun at the swimming pool.
After, we had burgers.

Sabrin Anno
Roehampton Church School, London

Journey To The Centre Of The Earth

One day I went to play with the ball in my pool.
I said to my friend, 'Would you like to go on an adventure with us?'
'OK,' she answered politely.
So before we went, we packed some food,
A water bottle and a watch to tell the time.
Off we went, first through a deep, dark cave,
Then a steep, cold mountain.
After five hours, we arrived at the deepest hole ever.
The ground started to shake.
So we went back home and lived the best life ever!

Nada Fermawi (6)
Roehampton Church School, London

Adventure Time

One day in the forest of adventure time
I was climbing up the bubblegum trees
And I grabbed all the bubblegum
And went on an adventure with Imogen,
Marissa and Indiana.
But Imogen, Marissa and Indiana fell over
So we went home and they slept for ages.

Holly Amos (7)
Roehampton Church School, London

The Zoo

Lions and leopards all around,
I was with my sister and my baby boy,
Before I went home I bought some bananas.

Samuel Asante-Nnuro (7)
Roehampton Church School, London

This Is All About The Sea

One day I was going to the sea
With Archi and Indiana.
We were going to have fun.
We were going to see dangerous animals:
Lions, tigers, snakes, elephants,
Loads to see.

Keira Waiters (7)
Roehampton Church School, London

Beach

I am going to eat
Really really good ice cream
I am going with my mum and dad
I can see the sun
I can hear seagulls
I can feel rocks
I can smell salt
I can taste ice cream.

Murlen Mufleh

Roehampton Church School, London

The Philippines

The Philippines is hot and sunny.
It is lovely because it's sunny.
I love the Philippines, even the weather.
I know this is amazing.
My grandparents will teach them their song
And it's funny.
If you go out don't wear your slippers. Ha, ha.

Jaden Bugnosen (7)

Roehampton Church School, London

Chelsea

I am going to play football
When it is a sunny day.
I am going with John Terry.
I can see John Terry on the football pitch.
I can sit in the chair and see Chelsea.
I am eating a sausage.

George Hayhoe (6)

Roehampton Church School, London

Beach

We were swimming in the sea
With a toy shark.
We were in a competition to see
Who could go to the end.
I won with Sidi.
We ate an ice cream with sprinkles on it.
We made a sand castle with a London flag.
We went home with a hot chocolate.

Jun Lee (6)
Roehampton Church School, London

At The Beach

One sunny morning I went to the beach with my mum.
When I got to the beach, the waves were really noisy
And the sun was really hot and bright.
The sun hurt my eyes.
I liked the seashells on the beach.
The seashells had lots of patterns on them.
The patterns on the seashells were pink and purple.
I love the beach.

Shania Goulbourne (6)
Roehampton Church School, London

Space

Hi, My name is Evie,
You might know me as your friend.
Today I am going on a mission to space
And I am going to jump off the moon.
A parachute will come out of my space suit
And I am going tomorrow morning.
I think I'm going to be famous.

Evie Harris

Roehampton Church School, London

Chelsea Stadium

I am going to score lots of goals
And do a cartwheel and a backflip.
I am going to take a free kick.
I am going to score a fantastic goal
And I am going to see Fernando Torres
And Etoro and Peter Cech.
I am going to see Terry.

Archi Lane-Wood (6)

Roehampton Church School, London

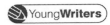

The Boxing Club

Me, Sidi and Archi went to a boxing club
And I won and I was famous.
Millions of people cheered my name.
When it was evening, I had a great party
And the next day I went on a big aeroplane to America.
In America it was so much fun.

Joshua K (6)
Roehampton Church School, London

Rihanna & Me

One day Rihanna asked me if
I would like to go to a disco.
I said yes.
When we got there, we danced
And ate lots of sweets.
When we went home
We dropped into bed and fell fast asleep.
The next day we went to disco the night away.

Margaret Amara (6)
Roehampton Church School, London

Adventure Time

One sunny day in Candy Kingdom,
Fin and Jake went to see Princess Bubblegum,
The princess of the Candy Kingdom.
Princess Bubblegum gave them a quest
To defeat the Ice King, the meanest king in the Candy Kingdom.
It never rains in Candy Kingdom, it is lovely there,
So that's why I want to go there.

Imogen Kelly (6)
Roehampton Church School, London

The Rainbow Land

One cold, winter's night
I got up and decided to go on a fascinating adventure
So I slipped on my trousers and top
And got on my skating jet ski and headed off
I dashed and got to a mystical land.

Then I saw something blue, prickly and tickly,
As I got closer I saw a prickly blue bush
It looked very still and I felt a thrill
It was Sonic.

Joshua Andrady (7)
St Joseph's RC Infant School, London

The Fairyland Adventure

One day I went to Fairyland with my brother
We found the sugar plum fairy
She said, 'Fairyland is in danger.'
A rat called King Rat is destroying Fairyland.
So I picked up a wand and I shrunk Fairyland but the wand didn't shrink me.
Suddenly I stepped on King Rat and everyone giggled with glee.

Annie O'Donnell (6)
St Joseph's RC Infant School, London

Future

One day the sun was bright
I made a time machine I went with Superman
It was a laugh
I can't remember a better dream.

I skated around and around
The snow was made of ice cream
I went to sleep and I said, 'Next time maybe!'

Jon-Reed Davies (7)
St Joseph's RC Infant School, London

Camp Alien

On day I went to Disneyland I wanted to find an alien dog
Suddenly I heard some crackling in the bushes
It was an alien dog and we had a little play
We didn't know where we were
But we landed in our spaceship and then we flew home.

Matthew Davey (6)
St Joseph's RC Infant School, London

Untitled

One day in the kingdom of lots of fairies
'I want a fairy too,' said the boy.
But it was too late said the kingdom
'I was so sad,' said the boy
'It's not too late, it was not too late,' said the kingdom
I put it in my pocket and I called it Sarah.

Isaiah Tabbal (6)
St Joseph's RC Infant School, London

Chocolate Land

One sunny morning I went to Chocolate Land
With my mum and dad
I saw shooting stars
I heard loud screaming
I could smell chocolate cream
I could taste sweets
I had fun playing there
I had candyfloss with my family.

Sarah Evans (7)

St Joseph's RC Infant School, London

Blackhole

I want to go to the black hole
I want to go with a chicken
I can see giant spiders
I can hear roaring
I can feel hot skeletons
I can smell green slime
I can taste turkey.

Then the deadly monsters came
One with no eyes
One with a sword in his brain
And one had a head cut off
Then they chased me.

Nicolas Venter (6)

St Joseph's RC Infant School, London

Untitled

One day I went to Jelly Baby Land
I went with my friend Ghost
It was really scary
I saw the biggest jelly baby
I could not believe my eyes
It was very big
I shrunk it
And I put it in my pocket
I ran home
I called it Bartosa.

James Davey (6)
St Joseph's RC Infant School, London

Adventure

One day I went to Sweet Land
I went with my ghost
We saw a castle made out of sweets
I saw red, yellow and blue colours
We came in but no one was there
Then I saw ice cream in a cup
I took the ice cream and I ate it.
Suddenly someone came in and I hid under the sofa
He had a gun
I saw the window and I got out of the building
I ran back home
I was hungry so I ate something.

Oliver Laurens (6)
St Joseph's RC Infant School, London

The Wonderful Sweet Land

One day I entered Sweet Land
I wanted to eat lots of sweet, sweets
It was amazing I couldn't believe my brown eyes,
When I saw candy on the trees,
Suddenly I saw the biggest sweet I've ever seen
I shrank it with a wand
And put it in my pocket.

Samara Ekwueme (6)
St Joseph's RC Infant School, London

Untitled

One day the alien gate opened.
I went into the gate,
I went to meet my friends
But they were not listening to me.
It was a good alien and it let me touch a rock
I was so happy, that I made friends with the alien.
It was such fun in space!
I put it in my car
I called that one Mars.

Jaden Aulis (6)
St Joseph's RC Infant School, London

A Trip To Fairy Land

Once I was in Fairy Land
I met the fairy queen
I saw some beautiful fairy dust
I picked it up and gave it to the queen
She said I could keep it!
I was very glad
She gave me wings too.

Rozi Bacso Antonio (6)
St Joseph's RC Infant School, London

I Found A Zombie

One day in Zombie Land
I wanted to find a zombie
It was scary with ripped clothes
I was scared
It was flappy and I ran away
I went in halfway
I got my wand and I put it in my pocket
I called it Joshua.

Rio Magali (6)
St Joseph's RC Infant School, London

My Adventure

One windy night I went to Monster Land
I went with my furry werewolf
I can see ghosts and vampires
I can hear scary laughing
I can feel furry werewolves
I can smell smelly feet
I can taste bat burgers
Then I will dance with the monsters
I will try the food
When I woke up I thought it was a dream.

Jessica Baldyga (7)
St Joseph's RC Infant School, London

A Journey To Marshmallow Land

One day, I went to Marshmallow Land
I was with my special dragon
I was walking on pink and white marshmallows
It tasted as sweet as strawberries
It was epic and amazing!
I put one in my pocket and
I called it Jeffery.

Joshua Rosabia (7)
St Joseph's RC Infant School, London

The Magic Land

One day I went to Iceland
I went with my dragon.
So I got on my dragon and flew into Iceland.
I went through the traps
Suddenly I saw a strange monster
It had two small legs and hands and it chased me
It ran quickly and then stopped and shouted
He shrunk and he followed me home
I saw a huge monster it was cooking
It chased me so Dad and Mum didn't cook
They were very happy that they didn't have to cook.

Kuba Hanzl (6)

St Joseph's RC Infant School, London

Sugar Rush

One day I went to Sugar Rush
And I wanted to find Penelope the candy girl
She had a green jumper and brown hair
I saw candy clouds.

Me and Penelope went in the café
And suddenly we saw big King Candy
He wanted to catch Penelope
But I stopped him.

Isabelle Howard-Garvey (6)

St Joseph's RC Infant School, London

97

Candy Land Adventure

Once I went to Candy Land
I went with a pink magical, sparkly fairy.
I could see soft roses around me.
I could hear the blue soft birds singing in the starlight.
I could feel ice cream frost with pies.
I could smell strawberry mountains.
I could taste sweets
I called my fairy to shrink it
And she came and she shrank it
And I went to my mum and dad
They were so impressed.

Mercielle Mpanzu (7)

St Joseph's RC Infant School, London

Fairy Land

One day I went to Fairy Land
I went with my mum and all my family
I wanted to find a fairy and it was beautiful and magical
It was so beautiful
I love fairies
It was such fun to see a fairy
I put it in my pocket
I called it Lilly.

Julia Sokolowska (6)

St Joseph's RC Infant School, London

Going To Sweet Land

One day I was going on an adventure
And it was going to be a fantastic day
I was going to Sweet Land
Maybe I can eat sweets in Sweet Land
It is going to be yummy
Finally I got there
I ate and ate and got full up
Then it was night
I had the worst dream ever
I was so scared
I was frightened.

Nicole Sebastiampillai (6)
St Joseph's RC Infant School, London

Ghost Hunters

One cold winter night
I went with my ghost dog
To a ghost house where there was a maze
It was very scary but it was so strange, we went in.

Me and my dog were not scared
There were lots of traps
But we found none because my dog knows the whole maze
Then we found a ghost but we didn't care.

Filip Rzeszotek (6)
St Joseph's RC Infant School, London

Sonic Volcano Race

On my birthday I woke up early
After I played on my Nintendo
When I was in the middle of
The race I got sucked in.

When I was in the game
My brother played on it
And he got sucked into the same place as me
I was amazed.

I called my car Land Scraper
And my brother called his car Black Lightning.

Michael Elegbede (6)
St Joseph's RC Infant School, London

Underwater Adventure

I went underwater
I saw a shark
The shark chased me but didn't catch me
We played hide-and-seek
Underwater

Kuba Koch (6)
St Joseph's RC Infant School, London

The Moon Adventure

I am in the park
And I want to go to the moon
I see an alien on the car
With my mum and dad

I can see aliens with red hair
They are cheerful
I can taste popcorn
I went down on the land with the alien.

James Johnston (6)
St Joseph's RC Infant School, London

Desert Adventure

One day I went to the desert with my friends
I saw Mario
I heard him walking
I saw and smelled coconuts
I tasted coconuts
My friends and me were on camels
And we ate the coconuts.

Ethan Udayar (7)
St Joseph's RC Infant School, London

Arsenal Stadium

Today I am going to Arsenal's stadium
Arsenal vs Tottenham
My dad is going with me
I am going to jump and score a goal
And Dad comes and there is a goal!
2-0 half time.
And I made myself the greatest player
In the whole wide world
Full time 7-0.

Michal Wilczynski (6)
St Joseph's RC Infant School, London

Moon Adventure

One day I went to the moon with Ellie
And when we got there we had chocolate cake with aliens
I nearly fell off the moon
It was so rocky.
I played hide-and-seek with Ellie
And the aliens.
Me and Ellie bounced back down to Earth.

Mia Wiseman (6)
St Joseph's RC Infant School, London

Chocolate Factory Adventure

One day in a chocolate factory
Me and Ellen loved chocolate
Yum-yum it was so delicious
Ellen and I found a chocolate stream
It was made of chocolate!
They had little men they were slimy men
It was so yummy
We took some chocolate home.

Amy Webster (6)

St Joseph's RC Infant School, London

Going To The Ocean

One day Maya and I went to the ocean
It was a good idea.
We saw dolphins,
We had lots of fun.
We found a magical seashell,
We turned into mermaids
We became friends with the sharks.

Lexie Horan (7)

St Joseph's RC Infant School, London

Video Game Mayhem

One day I was playing a video game
It was good, it was fun
We were playing with a bun.
I got sucked in with my mum and dad.

In a bang and a flash we were superheroes
With a flash and a dash we were immortal
I can see dust going along in the wind
I can hear lots of banging going on I can feel dust.

Finn Madigan (7)
St Joseph's RC Infant School, London

In Miss Donohue's House

One day I went to Miss Donohue's house
I wanted to know if she loved flowers
When I came to Miss Donohue's room
There were hundreds of flowers
I picked some of them up
And I named one George and one Amy.

Patrycja Sieczko (7)
St Joseph's RC Infant School, London

Sonic's Lost World

I went to help Sonic
We found magic powers
Then we decided to use them.
Leon's power is to stretch his body
Michael's power is to do high kicks
And my power is to drop bombs and help Sonic.

Liam Taruc (6)
St Joseph's RC Infant School, London

Robot Land Adventure

One day I woke up and went to get my friends
Leon, Michael, Michal, Daniel and Liam
We all went to Robot Land
We all went to get robot treasure.
Liam found a robot tree and shook it and it broke...
I saw lots of robots.
I heard moving parts of robots
I felt metal robots.
I smelt chocolate and I tasted chocolate.
Me and my friends found a big treasure chest -
It was robot treasure!
We all had a great time.

Jacob Tembo (6)
St Joseph's RC Infant School, London

105

Going To Paris

One day I went to Paris
With my Mum and Dad on a stunning plane.
I went to the Eiffel Tower
Right up to the top.
We went to a café
And we had smelly cheese and chocolate cake.

Omotorera Ogunade-Young (6)
St Joseph's RC Infant School, London

Going In To A Video Game

One day I was in a video game
I didn't know how I got there
I think that was him but I saw Melvin!

Melvin and I can see 100 sweets!
Melvin and I can hear screaming
We can feel superheroes!

We can smell fire
We can taste candyfloss
Me and Melvin are going to have candy.

Daniel Obi (6)
St Joseph's RC Infant School, London

106

Candy Land

One morning I got up early
And I caught a plane
And I went to Candy Land,
I could see candy,
I could hear a chocolate stream,
I could feel rock,
I could smell sweeties
And I could taste crisps.
Suddenly when I was not looking
A candy monster crept up to me and I saw it.

Anastasia Diamantopoulos (6)
St Joseph's RC Infant School, London

I Am Going In The TV

One day I was sitting watching TV
And I said, 'I am going in the TV,'
I took my dad with me
And when I got there I was so happy
I skipped, flipped and twirled.

I saw pink sand,
I heard the ocean
I felt the smooth rocks
And I tasted chocolate cake.

Amber Gachie (7)
St Joseph's RC Infant School, London

To Go To Mars

One day I woke up early and said to my best friend
'It is time to go to Mars.'
So I went with Lexie
We went on a rocket
And thirty minutes later we were there.
We landed, I saw green aliens
I heard a bouncing ball and I could feel smooth and cool Mars
And I smelled old cheese
I was scared
I told myself do not be scared
So we played with the aliens with a ball
We had cake, it was yummy
I said, 'Do you want to go home?'
Lexie said, 'No!'
We went home and went to bed.

Maya Chuderska (7)
St Joseph's RC Infant School, London

Aliens On Mars

One day I got a rocket
And put my unicorn in my pocket
I went in my rocket
And flew to Mars,
Then I ate lots of chocolate bars.
I met an alien and ate some cake
And when I got home
My alien was crazy!

Ellen Cooney (6)
St Joseph's RC Infant School, London

The Land Of Witches

One day I went to the sea
Guess what I can see?
Shells!
Then I saw a ship with aliens.
I went to the ship without asking
They flew me away.

They took me to the land of witches
I saw brown grass
And witches making hot brown grass
I made them stop
By giving them nice warm tea.

Ellie Chow (7)
St Joseph's RC Infant School, London

Disneyland Paris Adventure

One day I would like to go to Disneyland Paris
With my best friend Lexie
If I went to Disneyland
I wish I could turn into on of the Disney characters
I could trick people whenever I want.

A few minutes later I saw Cinderella
When I saw Cinderella Lexie went to see her
Me and Lexie were big fans of Cinderella
Me and Lexie got her autograph
It was really fun
We all had a nice laugh together.

Rachael Zannu (6)
St Joseph's RC Infant School, London

Going To Portugal

One day my mum woke me up and we were going to Portugal -
By rocket!
I felt excited!
The rocket smelt like a lemon cake
It was made out of sweets and cake.
It took us a day to get there!
We finally got to Portugal!
I saw a party with Rice Crispies
And lemon cake.

Melvin Samussone (6)

St Joseph's RC Infant School, London

The Beach Adventure

One day I went to the beach
Leon went with me
I saw a shark
It had sharp teeth and it bit my finger
I shouted loud
It was so loud.
I saw chocolate cake
Leon and I swam to the chocolate cake
It tasted like sweets.

Daniel Mbanzoulou (6)

St Joseph's RC Infant School, London

Magic Land

One day in Magic Land
I heard footsteps somewhere
Suddenly Clara came to tell me that her house is broken
We flew to her house
And rebuilt it with coloured bricks.
The house smelt like lime,
It tasted like orange cake
And it felt fluffy
The house looks better now.

Oreoluwa Oyefeso (7)
St Joseph's RC Infant School, London

Mungo

Mungo went to the library
There is Mungo
His book is about dinosaurs
It was his favourite book ever.

Marley Joseph Guerrero-Morris
St Joseph's RC Primary School, London

Me And The Turtles

Me and the turtles
Are going to fight
We hope the aliens are not going to attack the Earth
So we will fight tonight
We will save the Earth.

Conor White (7)
St Joseph's RC Primary School, London

The Space Wish

The sun sets, The moon rises, I look up to the sky,
I wish for some surprises.
Jupiter, Pluto and even Mars,
Looking at them brings me closer to the stars.
I look in the mirror and I see my face,
It makes me wish, I was in space.
Purple, green, yellow and red,
Aliens also need to go to bed.
The planets circle, The aliens go away,
I'll wake up and play with them another day. :-) xXx

Erika Feliciano-Varao (6)
St Joseph's RC Primary School, London

A South African Safari

As we drive in the heat of the hot African Sun
Me and my African family with the smell of the bush fire ahead
What is it we hear?
The roar of a ruthless lion calling his friends.
The sound of a lazy giraffe munching on mimosa leaves.
A cranky crocodile snapping its jaws on the banks.
The stomping of a slow elephant herd walking to the watering hole.
And a cheeky cheetah chasing a small gazelle.
After a long day driving off in the beautiful bush
We go back for a boerewors braai
There's nothing like a South African safari.

Elektra Curzi-Micallef (6)
St Joseph's RC Primary School, London

The Missing Diamond

I am all alone and ready wearing my adventure hat
I start walking through the deep dark forest
All that I could see is the moon
Then suddenly it seemed to be shining on the slimy gigantic tree
I stand and stare and there glitters a beautiful diamond
I ran to it, all that I could smell were rotten apples
Dropping from this ugly tree I quickly grabbed the diamond
I was surrounded by hundreds of bats I ran all the way home
Mum you would never guess what I got – the diamond.

Joseph Wright (7)
St Joseph's RC Primary School, London

The Adventure Of Louie, Lily And Ted

This year Louie got a very special birthday present
It was a rocket it came with three laser guns and astronaut suits
Next morning me, Lily and Teddy went to space
We just flew past the moon when suddenly a great big alien ship came
out of nowhere.
We came out of my rocket and attacked the aliens
Pow! Pow! Pow! take that for a change
We destroyed all the aliens
We had to fight the king alien *Pow! Pow! Pow!*
'We've killed him!' we cried
We landed in my garden safe and sound.

Louie Rawlings (7)
St Joseph's RC Primary School, London

113

Space Adventures With Pete And Neat

Scientist Pete and his bionic dog Neat lived on Planet Earth.
They loved to do experiments and eat lots of chocolate nerds!
One day, they got into their spaceship and flew all the way to the Milky Way.
They saw hot planets, red planets and freezing-cold fridge planets.
They saw prickly, pointy stars and heard loud, roaring rockets.
They tasted candy cane space dust and Milky Way stars.
They saw grumpy, green aliens.
They smelled stinky, mouldy moon-cheese.
But, that didn't matter because they had so much fun!
'Space is amazing!' said Scientist Pete.
'Let's go home and tell everyone.'

Gabriel Lampe (7)
St Joseph's RC Primary School, London

Sweety World

One day two wicked witches stole the rarest lolly.
The only person who knew about it was the Candy Princess
She was brave enough to get it back
While the witch got her spell book,
The princess got the rarest lolly
The wizard was surprised
So they celebrated by having a party!

Angelica Carrick-Andoh (7)
St Joseph's RC Primary School, London

Space

I jumped inside a spaceship and made its way to space.
I floated in the air and did not fear,
Jumping from one end to the next.
I saw a planet going around the big moon
Different stars shining brightly above Planet Earth.
It was calm, peaceful and magical
It was fun, I did not want to go home anytime soon.

Christian Castillo (7)

St Joseph's RC Primary School, London

My Daddy

My daddy is sweet, loving and kind.
He wakes me up in the morning with a shine.
I clean my room and take a bath
I brush my teeth and comb my hair
Daddy prepares my breakfast and takes me to school
He picks me up in the afternoon.
He teaches me reading, writing and maths
He tucks me into bed with prayers and lots of kisses
He hugs me tight and says goodnight.

Ricardo Diangkinay (6)

St Joseph's RC Primary School, London

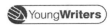

The Mummy's Adventure

One day Amy, Erika and I went to Egypt together
When we got there we went into the pyramids
When we were deep in the pyramids – *kaboom!*
A mummy appeared and then two and then a million
They started to follow us and we were petrified
We started to run as we had never run before
Then we went out to the sun to get a tan
And so did the mummies
So then they went onto the mummy place and so did we!

Estrella Del Pozo Jofré (7)
St Joseph's RC Primary School, London

The Scary Pirates And The Dolphin

Walking on the beach with my brother we saw a pirate ship
Water splashing on the sea
The dolphin was swimming near the ship
The pirates grabbed the big net and
Were lining up waiting for their turn to catch the dolphin.
We swung the vine, then dropped into the pirate ship
We shouted, 'Put your hands up you scary pirates
And let the dolphin go!'
They let the dolphin go free
We shouted, 'Hooray! Hooray!'

Adriel Mekonenn (6)
St Joseph's RC Primary School, London

Skylands

As I closed my eyes and awoke with a thud
I found myself stuck in mud.
It was up to my neck and I had no hope
When my dad appeared he had a piece of rope.
As I looked around all I could see were Skylanders everywhere
Coming for me.
My dad pulled me free and we started to run
There were Skylanders everywhere, this wasn't much fun.
We were stuck on Skylands, a magical place
Where Skylanders ruled the human race.
We kept on running and fell off a cliff
I started to scream as I thought I was dead
And then I awoke safe in my bed
It was just a dream.

James Graney (7)
St Joseph's RC Primary School, London

Searching Bouncy Ball

We are aliens,
We are searching for our ball
We are going to the sun
We can smell the chocolate cake
We can hear lovely music
Space is a lovely place!

Antonio Borrelli (7)
St Joseph's RC Primary School, London

117

Magic Land Palace

Once upon a time in Magic Land
In the palace there was a girl named Alice
Who liked to eat lollies.
Boy, boy and his very little toy
Walked to Drew and said, 'I love you.'
Mum and Dad went to the forest
And they said hello to their friend called Norris.

Drew Ross (6)
St Joseph's RC Primary School, London

Untitled

One day two big boys went to space
In the rocket in space
Time to find aliens on Mars
They talked to an alien
And there were lots and lots of stars.

Johnnie Healey (5)
St Joseph's RC Primary School, London

Best Friends

When the moon is shining bright
Me and you will have a good night
We will have a midnight feast
And watch Beauty and the Beast
In the morning we can play in the park
All day long before it gets dark
Me and you are best friends
Until the very end.

Kiki Cartwright (6)
St Joseph's RC Primary School, London

The Princess, The Prince And The Bodies

In the forest there was a princess and a prince
And they were having a nice time.
But suddenly, the mean king came with his assistant.
And mean king took the princess
And the prince told his assistant to go and get the princess.

Silvia Rona (6)

St Joseph's RC Primary School, London

Arsenal Won The FA Cup Final

We are in the dressing room, we are excited.
Come on lads we can do it
We walked down the long dark tunnel
We ran onto the pitch and the crowd went wild
Come on Arsenal, come on Arsenal
Whistle . . .
The game kicks off
There is a nasty slide tackle
Number 11 took a shot and he scored in the top right-hand corner
What a beautiful goal
It has been 90 minutes
The whistle blows and Arsenal wins the trophy.

Eddie Wright (6)

St Joseph's RC Primary School, London

Cheetah

There was a cheetah sitting on Peter
His name was also Peter
So it was Peter and a cheetah called Peter
Peter always liked to bounce and cheetah always liked to bounce too.
They bounced to the zoo and they bounced to the park
They bounced in the morning and they bounced in the dark.

Bernu Kotowska (7)
St Joseph's RC Primary School, London

Forest Adventure

In the forest there were a lot of animals
Such as fox, wolf, bears, monkeys, tigers, owls
A fox that goes, *wow-wow-wow!*
Wolf goes *whooooo*
Bear goes *faaaaw*
Monkey goes *ooh-ooh, ooh-ooh*
Tiger goes, *rowl, snarl, roar, whoof*
Owl goes *tu-whit-tu-whoo*
All the animals were created by God.

Rakeem Mckoy (7)
St Paul's RC Primary School, London

Sweet Land

I met a fairy with a head band,
Who took me to Magic Land.
We flew across the sugar sky
And saw a lovely butterfly.
We landed on the pink cupcake
And jumped on the red pancake.
The birds were singing
And we were swinging.
Everything was so sweet
And we had a treat.
It was a big feast
But it ceased!

Izabela Segmen (6)
St Paul's RC Primary School, London

I Went To The Jungle

In the jungle I saw a tiger
And he looked angry like a fire
He bit my ears and smelled my pie
He look at my pie and then ate it all
He wanted more so I gave him a cake
And I ran to the car and went home
I shouted every night and saw stars and fell asleep.

Roshien Jude Roshan (7)
St Paul's RC Primary School, London

Pyramids

Pyramids, pyramids I want to see you
And I want to ride on a big camel.
I want to go and have some fun
But going to the desert is so, so hot
It gives us fun all the time
I like going into the pyramids
And to see all that is in them.
But there is so much to see in there
And there are more pyramids to see
And everywhere there are bigger ones
And you can go to the top of them.

Kendrick Luciano (6)
St Paul's RC Primary School, London

In The Jungle

Roar, roar, scary lion
I am not scared of you
Roar, roar, scary lion
I am going to play with you.
Roar, roar, scary lion
We are going to have fun.
Roar, roar, scary lion,
We are not going to tell mum.

Antosh Grabiec (6)
St Paul's RC Primary School, London

Magical Jungle

I went to a magical jungle
And I saw a fairy
That was very hairy.
Then I saw a tiger
That was yawning and then roaring.
I saw a cat on a magical mat.
Then I saw an elephant that jumped then hummed.

Aliyah Vita (6)
St Paul's RC Primary School, London

I Went To Space

I went to space and I saw a hairy, scary, furry baboon
We jumped to Mars and the funny, crazy baboon
Was being very funny because he was exited
The baboon was being very, very funny
And the funny, hairy, scary baboon was being so funny
That he made us go to the moon
And we saw that we had to go to bed, so we did!

Ela Pernavaite (6)
St Paul's RC Primary School, London

The Dinosaur Adventure

Once upon a time I was hunting for dinosaurs
I went outside and saw a dinosaur
At the end of his body was a long spiky tail
He was stomping his ginormous feet on the floor
The ground was cracking and nearly disappearing beneath his feet.

Lazar Manev (6)
St Paul's RC Primary School, London

123

The Magical Faraway Tree

Me and my friends all went to the magical faraway tree
And we saw a bat and she had a silly hat.
She showed us a ladder that was made out of bladder
It was quite disgusting too
We climbed up the bladder ladder
The bat was behind us, the one with the silly hat
When we got to the top
There was a land called Humble Mumble Land
If you don't know why Humble Mumble Land had such a silly name
Well then I would need to tell you.
Humble Mumble Land got its name
Because everybody humbles and mumbles so much
As we were walking along we sang a silly song.
When we got tired we went back to our safe, cosy, warm homes
And guess what?
We were just in time for dinner.
As for the bat with the silly hat
Well she was also in time for her delicious dinner too.

Amira McLoughlin (7)
St Paul's RC Primary School, London

Magical Zoo

First I am going to see the chimpanzee that is lazy and crazy
And then I am going to see the monkey that is funny and silly
After that I am going to see the tiger that is orange and that has black stripes
And he is silly and funny.
After that I am going to see the leopard that is silly and crazy and lazy.
At the end I am going to see the funny and silly elephant.

Sarah Woznica (6)
St Paul's RC Primary School, London

124

The Magical Forest

Two little girls went to the park after school for relax time
When it was time to go home, they got lost
Two little girls were very sad they ran around trying to get out
Suddenly they saw something shining so they went and chased it
Before they lost it
They arrived in a magical place
They saw a gold treasure box, two lovely fairies and a beautiful
mermaid too!

Deo (6)
St Paul's RC Primary School, London

Magic Land

Me and my mum had fun in Magic Land
And we were singing
My mum said she wanted to buy a ring and it was very amazing and
shiny
It was blue with diamonds and the diamonds could fall out
Me and my brother saw a big pool where people could swim
We had great fun in the end.

Arleni Male (7)
St Paul's RC Primary School, London

Tumble In The Jungle

I fell into the jungle with a loud tumble many years ago
All I heard were big, loud footsteps
As I ran through the deep jungle
I met my friend the bear
Running fast we went to the land of the dinosaur
As we got closer I heard a *roar! Roar!*
Jumping into the swamp we started to fight into the night
It started to rain so we vanished back into the deep, dark jungle.

Jake D.w. (6)
St Paul's RC Primary School, London

The Magical Zoo

In the zoo I saw a lion and it was yawning and roaring.
Then I saw lots of oak, old, tall, big trees
There was honey also on the stony, rocky, old path
There were very shiny bricks.
Next I felt a fairy
So I looked at the fairy and it was very hairy
After I saw a funny, happy, nice monkey
So I gave it an enormous banana
He cut the banana into pieces and he gave me some
He gave his babies some and he left some for himself.

Valentina Guzman
St Paul's RC Primary School, London

Theme Park Adventrue

We went to an old theme park,
We needed to get the key,
We needed to catch the fire monster,
'But how?' said Leo.
We went to the middle of the park,
We threw a stick at him
We did it!
We went home!

Timothy Wellington (7)
Vita Et Pax School, London

The Adventure Of Dinosaurs

One day we found a time machine,
So we pushed the button,
And we flew off!
We arrived in a mysterious land
Full of dinosaurs
We crept carefully
We bumped into a dinosaur on the way
I wasn't scared because he was friendly.
'Hello,' he said, 'I'm Rex!'
'I'm Alannah!'
We made friends
And we skipped home.

Alannah Doyle (6)
Vita Et Pax School, London

Our Volcano Quest

Dom, Tim and I are on a quest to find the sword of doom
And the golden shield
But trouble is ahead
We have to get past a live volcano,
So I swam down because I'm made of fire
So the others froze it with their ice guns,
We got down and found them,
But a group of ninjas came up to us and had a battle
I burnt some, and they froze them
We got the sword and shield and went home.

Alexander Richmond (6)

Vita Et Pax School, London

My Dolphin Adventure

I was swimming one day
and a nice dolphin came to see me.
She said, 'Do you want a ride!'
'Yes I do. Can you take me to a rock
and I will sit there!'

Emily Westmore (6)

Vita Et Pax School, London

My WW2 Adventure

I went back in time
Flying my time machine
We travelled back to WW2
At first we went on a train
We had target practice
We turned into soldiers
We joined the war
We battled Hitler
We captured him
We put him in jail.

John-Paul Kendrew (6)
Vita Et Pax School, London

The Treasure Chest

I went to look for treasure
I dug underground
I found the treasure chest
Full of golden, glittery nuggets.

Christopher Demetri (6)
Vita Et Pax School, London

Princess Adventure

I'm a princess on the ground
I took a boat for a ride,
It was fun, I had a bun,
But then things went wrong,
I crept through the garden,
My necklace sparkled,
I smiled with a grin,
A pocket flew down
But a wicked professor spoke,
Got me and my friend,
He put us in a net,
'Help! Help!' I said.

Amalya-Lovett Antwi-Agyei (6)

Vita Et Pax School, London

Dolphin Adventure

I floated through the sea
My dolphin tail behind me,
In the distance I saw Grace
Behind her was a shark
'Grace, come here before he eats you!'
Grace turned around and swam to the shore.

Daniella Panteli (6)

Vita Et Pax School, London

A Battle With A Giant

One day I went for a walk,
And found a massive castle
I didn't know what was inside
It was a giant,
I came face to face with him
Then we had a battle
And I won!

Zak Rahman-Cook (6)
Vita Et Pax School, London

Chess Adventure

Once upon a time was a chessboard
There were chess pieces on the board
I was the queen
My friend was the pawn,
Suddenly the black pieces attacked
The white fought back
Then the white won
'Yes!' said me and Joseph
We won!

Mario Georgiou (6)
Vita Et Pax School, London

Going Into Space

I am fed up of not knowing about space
I told my mother
So I am going to orbit all the planets,
Oh is it time for the picnic yet?
It's three o'clock, it's time for lunch!
Yum yum it's delicious jam sandwiches
What a beautiful sight I saw.

Neriah Chanda (6)
Vita Et Pax School, London

My Time Machine Adventure

We're going back in a time machine
Oh where's the mime?
I think he's down the line
He floated into space with a spaceship
And we will go and get him through the Milky Way.
We could not see him
He was camouflaged on the moon with a prune
'Where's the mime?' I asked.
'I don't know but I think he's got a prune.'

Dominic Polzone (6)
Vita Et Pax School, London

My Adventure On The Titanic

Me and John-Paul
Are going to sea
On the Titanic
I hope he will be as happy as me!

Floating away we saw a bay
We slept on the bay for half a day
We stood on the bay
Not for long

But I was wrong
John-Paul had to sing a song.

Rhianna Morgan (7)

Vita Et Pax School, London

Adventure Poem

One day two people and two dogs went for a walk.
They saw two robbers in a tree.
They had lots of guns,
So did we.
The robbers ran away,
The dogs ran after them.

Joseph Mills-Lamptey (7)

Vita Et Pax School, London

133

Quest Adventure

Me, Shourya and Lep are on a quest,
We are on a quest to save Princess Esmerelda
And then a monster caught us
But we escaped from him
He chased us
So we ran to find shelter,
Shourya said, 'I see a cave!'
In the cave was Esmerelda
We ran into the cave
Then we saved her.

Sai Patel (7)
Vita Et Pax School, London

The Sea

I wondered through the sea
My mermaid tail behind me.
What a good day,
I said to the sea
I wish I had friends
With me.

Zoe Henry (6)
Vita Et Pax School, London

Mermaid Adventure

I am swimming in the sea
And just then I feel strange
It's Daniella
My friend from above.
I giggled as I said,
'Would you like a ride?'
'Oh yes,' she yelled
'I always wanted to have one.'
So I said, 'Let's go!'
We swam and swam
Until I said
'You must go back to land!'

Maria-Nephele Gkiaouri (6)

Vita Et Pax School, London

Untitled

We are going to the jungle
We are going to find a tiger
With Dom, Tim and Leo
We touched the tiger
The tiger was calm
Then we had some lunch
Then we went home.

Akinlolu Oduyemi (6)

Vita Et Pax School, London

135

The Chess Board

I went to the chess board
I transformed into a piece,
I was a knight,
I did not like pieces moving around
It was allowed in chess
It was fun.

Leo Garcia (6)

Vita Et Pax School, London

Quest Adventure

One day me and my friends went on a quest
We needed to get the treasure
We needed to defeat the boss.
'First we should save the princess.'
'Let's go,' said Lep.
'Wait, we need a map!' said Sai.
'We've found a map,' said Lep.

Shourya Mondal (7)

Vita Et Pax School, London

Our Monster Battle Adventure

I was one day playing with Rhianna and Sai,
When a small rocket came floating by
We jumped into the rocket and floated away,
Soon after that we landed in Monster Land
But the king monster found us and took us into the fighting valley
Soon after Rhianna had a plan she said
'I'll shake my fire bubble bottle and it'll kill all the monsters!'
'Great idea!'
So Sai and I hid
While Rhianna went secretly round the monsters
Making a big bubble of fire as she went
Until all the monsters were dead.
'We won!' we exclaimed.
So we jumped into our rocket
We floated back into Rhianna's garden
Where we were playing
Just in time for tea.

Mary-Ellen Dyson (6)
Vita Et Pax School, London

137

The End

of the
Adventures

Information

We hope you have enjoyed reading this book – and that you will continue to enjoy it in the coming years.

If you're a young writer who enjoys reading and creative writing, or the parent of an enthusiastic poet or story writer, do visit our website www.youngwriters.co.uk. Here you will find free competitions, workshops and games, as well as recommended reads, a poetry glossary and our blog.

If you would like to order further copies of this book, or any of our other titles, then please give us a call or visit www.youngwriters.co.uk.

Young Writers
Remus House
Coltsfoot Drive
Peterborough
PE2 9BF

01733 890066 / 898110

info@youngwriters.co.uk